Leon Parrish was born on 14 July 1946, in Hunslet, Leeds; the hub of foundries, glass works, pits, pubs, and more pubs. Where all its people were poor, but happy and they just got on with their lives.
Keep smiling.

To my ma'am for all her sacrifices to make my life complete.
To my wife, Patricia, for the love.
And to my family and friends (worldwide), without who I would be nowt.

Leon Parrish

THE STORY OF LORD LEON AND THE GAFFER ABOVE

OBSERVED BY THE BOY FROM THE TIN BATH

AUSTIN MACAULEY PUBLISHERS™

LONDON * CAMBRIDGE * NEW YORK * SHARJAH

A CIP catalogue record for this title is available from the British Library.

ISBN 9781398438897 (Paperback)
ISBN 9781398438903 (ePub e-book)

www.austinmacauley.com

First Published 2022
Austin Macauley Publishers Ltd®
1 Canada Square
Canary Wharf
London
E14 5AA

To all of the wonderful people that we have met on our train journey over our lifetime, we thank you all.

Table of Contents

1. Ups After Downs

A Car Fit for a Lord

Just like Toad of Toad Hall, I couldn't take my eyes off the magnificent automobile that I had just spotted in a thumbnail-sized photo in the Yorkshire Post.

My heart had been stolen by the 21-foot-long Buckingham! Created in 1985 by eight Aston Martin Lagonda craftsmen in Buckinghamshire, it was truly magnificent. The 2.7-tonne beast had a swan mascot in solid brass. It was fit for a lord, and I wanted to be lord of that car. I bid for it over the phone, and bought it unseen. I was left with one tiny problem: it was too large for my garage! No problem for Lord Leon. I just decided, okay – I'll build a new one!

Lord of the Manor

Always up for a laugh, I had become Lord of Methley between 1998 and 2000. It was fantastic fun being a lord and it was great having that title on my passport, and credit card. When the press came to interview Pat and I about our new position in life, they asked Pat what it was like being Lady of Methley. Her reply was very true: "I've always been a lady!"

The title, Lord Methley, goes back to the Domesday Book and its documents are contained in the Archives library, in Leeds. My title meant that I could hold a market in the thriving Leeds village of Methley. The title was granted by the Earl of Mexborough after the Norman Conquest, and comes with the right to appoint a High Sheriff and bailiff.

When I went over to America, they loved having an English lord over there. Once they knew I was a lord, they bent over backwards to ensure my stay was exceptionally good. When I looked out of the window of my room, in the luxury hotel in Nashville, it overlooked a freeway. However, when I told them I was Lord Methley, from England, they immediately moved me to a better suite, and sent champagne up to the room!

Don't worry; it wasn't all self-indulgent glory, because as Lord Methley, I got invited to support charity work. For example, I was proud to present twelve computers to young people at the Head Start project at the Hunslet club.

After a bit of ribbing from my mates, I decided it was time to pass the title on. It was given to a race horse, and I became good mates with Geoff, the new owner of my title. I might like to consider buying it back one day! Anyway, once a lord, always a lord – well, at least in the hearts of my family and friends! In my business, it can be a bit distracting to be addressed as Lord Methley. I decided it was time for me to leave the aristocracy. The press ran an article about me wanting to sell it on, and that very night it was sold.

My sons proved that I am still a lord in their hearts, because they both wrote a letter to the press when one reader complained about me, a commoner, becoming a lord through purchase. Their words meant the world to me: "Our Dad has earned respect from all walks of life, not just for all his charity work but also his whole outlook on life itself. Dad has a saying, 'All the money in the world belongs to the working man.' We say if the working man earns it, he can spend it how he likes, and that includes titles, lordships, or whatever. We are very proud of our father."

Well done sons, because after that, the reader changed his tune and wrote in again with an apology! It was heart-warming to read other letters of support for me as Lord, including the kind words, "Leon did not have to buy a title to become a lord, when he is something better, a true gentleman."

Lord Leon

So, Lord Methley stepped down to become Lord Leon, lord of his family instead. My greatest treasure will always be my family. Some lords might recall the days they made their fortune. Here's mine!

On 24th July 1997 at 16.20 pm, my grandson Macaulay and I were playing with play dough. Don't worry, he was two then, not the quarter-of-a-century-old man he is now! He suddenly stopped what he was doing, looked straight at me with his big blue eyes and smiled, saying, "Love you, my Grandad." This was the best moment of my life. That was the best treasure Lord Leon ever found.

Roots

I'm proud of my roots, born in Hunslet on 14th July 1946. My motto in life is, "You gotta graft for it." That's the main message, really, from my story. Although I've done well in life, I worked my socks off to achieve it. Having said that, I acknowledge that I've had my fair share of angel dust sprinkled on me from the Gaffer Above. You will see the many times that the Gaffer, up there, has looked out for me and mine.

I was given the name Leon Michael Davies Parrish by Annie, the most amazing mother, who I know, you will come to admire as much as all the many, many, many folks who knew her in life did.

My mam's sister, Violet, died in a tragic accident. Hers was the first funeral I ever attended. She had always wanted a son called Michael, hence my name. Thankfully she was blessed with her own son, before the accident, so now I have a cousin, Michael! Davies was my original father's name.

I researched the history of the name Parrish. The earliest recorded instance was in Yorkshire in 1379: Willelmus de Parysch. There is a record of Thomas de Parysch in 1379, too. The Parrish coat of arms is three unicorn heads, and the motto is, "While I have breath, I have hope." I have always believed the phrases, "determination" and "hard work," sum my family up, and I admit we are optimistic.

The Boy from the Tin Bath

So, who is this boy from the tin bath? It was me. As a child, I came from a very poor home. Annie, my wonderful mam, always found a way to feed us all, and she kept us clean, but I don't really know how. I was born just outside South Leeds, in Hunslet. We lived in a back-to-back house with a toilet down the street and that tin bath, which it took an age to fill and heat, by the fire. My mam had me, the eldest boy, my sister, Faye, who was seven years older than me, and my brothers Barrie, Trevor, Peter and Keith, all in that tiny house. Later, when our Hunslet house was knocked down, we moved to Belle Isle where I got my own bedroom! Mam had Roy and Paul there. Sadly, Roy got off my train some stops back.

Cedric Parrish was Faye's father. Her dad came home from war and died from pneumonia. Years later, my mam was working in munitions and met the boss who'd come up from Swansea. He took her out, dated her and nine months later, I was born! In those days, that was a big no-no. He was a married man with a family in Swansea, so I've never met him. In later years, I considered searching for him, but it wouldn't really be fair to open up a can of worms in case his other family knew nothing of me.

My mam would take me to Leeds Town Hall each Saturday. We'd walk, as she had no money for a tram. She'd sit me down on one of the stone lions outside, go in, and come out crying. This would happen every Saturday. Why? Mam was always hopeful that some maintenance would have been paid by him, and she would make this journey, in hope, every week. He never paid a penny, and eventually she stopped going.

I'll Save You, Mam.

Three years after I came along, Mam married Bill Chadwick, and they had another six lads. Bill was a fabulous fitter but he'd hardly ever go to work. The gaffers used to come round asking him to go, and set a machine up for them. He'd take the money, promise to turn up, and then go straight to the pub!

He was an alcoholic, so we never had owt. Silly little things stick in my mind, like my memory of all the Irish workmen digging away on a job near us. Obviously, there were no JCB diggers in those days, and I'd go and watch them slaving away. They'd say, "Will you go, kid, and get us summat from the shops?" They'd want pop, stuff like that, so they'd give me a halfpenny for doing it. I'd take the old bottles and get coppers back for those too. I stored all my wages up in a little jar.

Then I started buying bottles of orange and watered them down, and they were happy to buy it off me, so I made about two pence per bottle. My little jar was getting rather heavy but then, you guessed it, like a magpie stealing eggs, Stepfather Billy found my little stash of three penny bits and pennies. I went upstairs one day to put summat in it and it was empty, and he was in the pub spending my earnings. I was gutted.

I got a paper round, before school, and I used to deliver the newspapers on my bogie; a wooden cart with four wheels. One day, on the way back from my newspaper round, I looked down and spotted a ten-shilling note. I was drenched, absolutely wet through, as was my discovered treasure. I carefully prised the sodden note off the pavement and put it on my chest; it was so precious I had to keep it safe. I raced straight into the house, shouting, "Mam, mam!" She was delighted, but the vulture hovered over me. "What you got there then?" He grabbed it off my hand and put it on the mantle to dry. I knew what was coming as he went off to shave and wash. Yes, straight out with my ten-bob note. I was gutted again, but it taught me a lesson: to never tell anybody anything in future.

I wasn't bitter, as I don't think I had an ounce of bitterness in me. He was cruel to me, since I wasn't his son. He used to sit me in a corner and would tell me not to move for an hour. When I was about 13, I remember, he knocked seven bells out of me. He wasn't very good to my mother, either. He used to bray her. Once I jumped on his back, screaming, "Leave my mam alone!" I got a black eye and a busted lip, but I beat him in that fight. After that, he never touched me nor my mam again. He still argued, like mad, but he never touched us again! Strangely, when he died, I was sad like I'd lost a dad. Well, he was the only dad I knew.

Extended Family

One special memory from my childhood is meeting my mam's family from Staley Bridge. It was a huge adventure going on the train to meet them. They all gave me half-crowns, which, of course, I gave to my mam to pay for the train.

We used to visit Grandad Harry every Sunday morning and take him some shopping. He used to give me a tanner but my brothers just got three penny bits, so I guess I was the favourite! He sat in his chair by the fire, flat cap on, shirt sleeves rolled up to the elbows, waistcoat on and a big thick leather belt round his middle. He was a great grandad, who used to have a horse and trap. He'd charge kids a penny for a ride, and he'd grow his own food in an allotment and sell it. Maybe I got my entrepreneurial skills from him! He used to play his concertina for a sing-song with us, and if any of us lads were getting rowdy, he'd take off his belt and snap it as a warning.

My mother's mum, my grandma, was also called Annie, but sadly she died when I was five. I remember my grandad picking me up to kiss her in the coffin.

Mam told me that, once, when I was in my pram, a neighbour said, "When Leon smiles, he looks like he doesn't belong here." My mam said that she hadn't a clue what the woman meant at the time, but as the years passed, she claimed she understood. "The more you grow, the more I think you are meant for better things." I can tell you now, there never was nor ever will be better things than my family, but I have been gifted with a life of blessings.

Annie and Harry Webster, my grandparents

10.5

Me, age 6

Me with my brother Peter

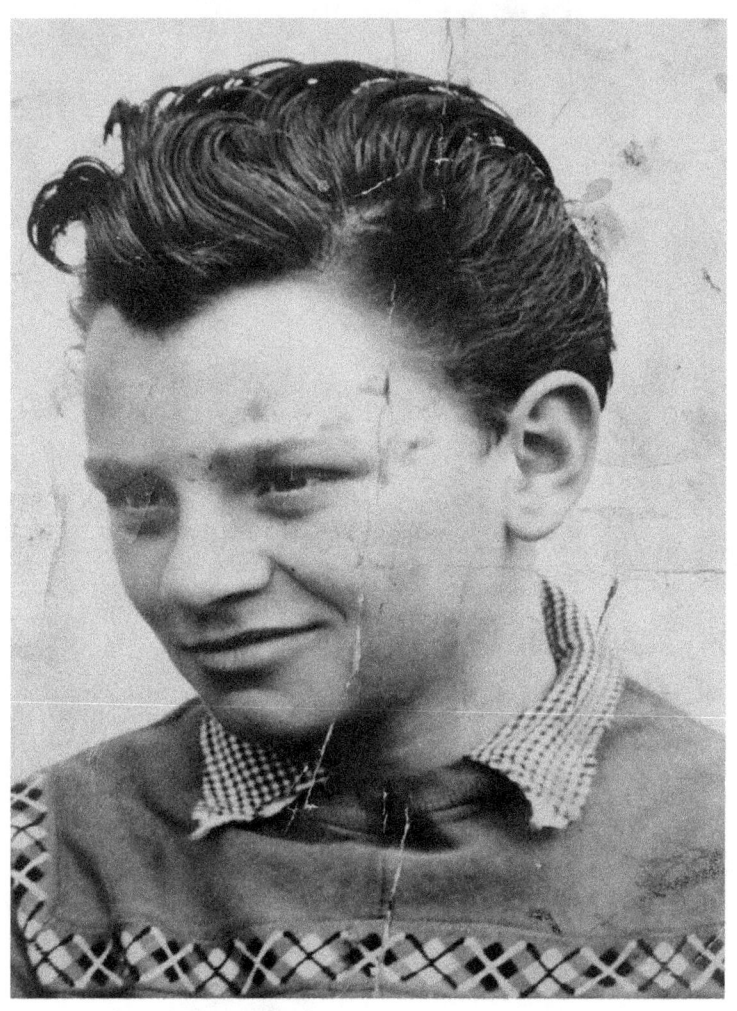

Poor but happy

Early family fun

My mam Annie

Hunslet born and bred

2. Foundation Stones

Introducing the Gaffer Above

I don't go to church, but I believe in the Gaffer Above and Jesus. When my stepfather's behaviour became intolerable, my mam left home and took all us four lads with her. We lived in Hunslet vicarage. The vicar, Mr Wilkes, and his wife had children of their own, so as you can imagine, it was a busy household. My mam used to clean for him and in those days, vicars were vicars and practised what they preached. He took in my mam and five kids for five months, free of charge. We went to church and Hunslet Baptist Sunday school. All I experienced stuck with me, and I still believe in my God. I believe it is He who sent angels to look after me, after a few words with my mam!

Childhood Christmas

Christmas was always very happy. It was so exciting to receive an apple and a tangerine. A tanner, a silver sixpence, was always pushed into the skin of the apple. How mam afforded it all I'll never know, as there were so many of us kids, and we all got a bag of sweets too, plus other bits and bobs in pillowcases. We'd sit around the Christmas tree while Mam tickled away on the ivories, and we all sang our hearts out. We'd had a barrel of laughs making the paper decorations to dress the tree. My mam always made Christmas so special, so maybe that's why I love it so much now, spending it on our cruises, partying away.

Schooldays

As a child, I attended Low Road School. I remember one of the teachers came to school one day in a brand-spanking-new white Morris 1000 Estate. It highlighted, for me, the contrast between those who had and those who didn't, like my family. It also helped to ignite my interest in motors. I loved cars, but when I was a kid there weren't a lot about. My friend, Wilfred, had an uncle who used to take us out in a fab car. I'll never forget those rides.

My mam discovered a place you could get good second-hand clothes from, for free! She dragged me along. Staring up at me were a pair of brand-new brogues. Amazingly, they were my size. The girl behind the desk read my face and said, "You want those shoes, don't you?" I was about 13, and I'd never had a brand-new pair of shoes in my life. I was over the moon, and when I got home, I polished those shoes until I could see my face in them. I was as proud as punch when I wore them to school. I'd been going into school with sandals with no soles, so I can't explain the feeling those shoes gave me. I felt so important.

There was a rugby player at school, two years older than me. He came up to me and he said, "Parrish, let us look at those shoes." So, being a bit naïve, I put my foot forward to show them off. The toe-rag jumped on my foot! It killed, but the real pain was when I looked down. He'd dinted my shoes. A red mist came over me. I jumped on him and attacked him. He was tons bigger than me, but I beat the crap out of him. Teachers came running and dragged me off him. I was crying with rage. I was sent to the head teacher and got dismissed from school for a week. Nowt happened to him! I still loved those shoes and tried to push the dint out, but the leather still cracked. Nobody ever tried to set on me again after that. I nearly killed the lad!

Mam was good at managing her money. Like I said, she sorted out second-hand clothes for us, and she used to go to Mr Mell's grocers in Hunslet because he would take tick. He was so laid back about getting paid. There was also 1001 bargains shop selling anything you could want. I bought my first teddy boy coat from there, a light blue jacket with black velvet cuffs and collar.

One day there was a massive sports day at Roundhay Park, and one of the teachers asked me if I'd like to earn five pounds, which was a tremendous amount of money in those days. I had to sell programmes all around the park. I guess my entrepreneur skills from my pop-selling days reignited, because I sold hundreds of programmes.

I was a good swimmer, especially in back stroke. I couldn't do the turn at the end of the pool though, which gave those who could an advantage. The head teacher didn't like me. He didn't like any kid who didn't play rugby, nor any kid who wore scruffy clothes. My mam had sewn a huge old coat button on my shirt neck as she couldn't find any other, and he pulled me up for that in front of everyone. Anyway, one day, totally out of the blue he announced, "There's an inter-schools' swimming competition and you're chosen to represent school." He gave me an address. I didn't have a clue how to get there, and I had no bus fare. Persevering Parrish decided to collect scrap from the local tip to sell. I reckoned I could get a half crown for my tram fare. The policeman who caught me thought otherwise and escorted me home! When Mam had seen the policeman off, she told me to walk. She drew me a map for the six-mile journey. I eventually got there, but I'd missed the race! A kid I'd beaten before had won it.

The next day I was petrified of what the head would say!

"Typical, Parrish," he stormed before striding away. He was pretty annoyed when I went through the hall, where he was teaching a class, to get to the toilet. "Parrish, you've not paid your dinner money," he yelled. Everyone in his class turned and sniggered. I looked straight at him as I told him what he already knew: "Sir, I'm on free dinners." He gave me the cane for being sarcastic, but it was well worth it for those brilliant school dinners where you got loads on your plate.

I was quite used to the cane or slipper. We went to another school to do woodwork. At playtime, once, I went to the local shop and got an orange. The teacher had said that we weren't allowed out of school, and on my return, he'd grassed me up. I got called out in assembly for the cane on each hand.

I didn't like reading books (and I still don't) but I liked comics. Dan Dare, Beano and Mythical Thor all grabbed my interest. Thor actually inspired me to write a great story in an exam where, for once, I actually got a high mark. Being such a livewire, I reckon the teachers should have redirected my energies on the stage. I'd have loved to have a leading role, but I did get to star as a reindeer in one Christmas play. I was chuffed with my part; being able to kneel and nod my head as my proud mam looked on! The scruffy poor kids, like me, had to sit at the back of classrooms, and in a class of 50 we couldn't hear a thing, so we just gave in to firing ink pellets at each other!

One frightening memory I recall is when I picked up an injured bird in the playground. I put it in my desk. The teacher was boring me, so I thought I'd see how my bird was. It tried to hop out of my desk. As I reached to grab it, the lid fell on my bird! "Parrish, what are you banging your desk for?" came the angry voice of my teacher. She ordered me to go to the Horrific Headmaster. I was crying, and it was the only time he showed me compassion. He took the squashed bird out of the desk, sent me home and said he'd forget the incident!

When I was fourteen, they closed Low Road school down to the older kids. We were moved to a brand-new school at Belle Isle called Belle Isle Secondary Modern, and I blossomed there. Every twenty minutes you'd hear the pips. These meant, move on to your next lesson. The short spells kept me interested. When I went there, my exam results zoomed up and I came second in the first exams I sat, rather than my usual second from bottom position!

We had some laughs. In cross country running we passed my home, 202 Middleton Road, so we went back to my house for food and drink, and waited for the rest on their way back!

Leisure times

We went to the picture house every Saturday. Cowboy and Indian films were our favourite. You'd find us running up and down the aisle, copying our heroes, as we chased around waiting for the film, but as soon as the music started everyone immediately sat down. We adored the Lone Ranger and Tonto. Dan Dare and The Clay Men were my favourite films to watch.

The first time I ever saw the sea was at Bridlington when I was14 years old. A neighbour took me in his motorbike side car, and I just couldn't believe it when I spotted the ocean. I ran straight into the waves. That was an amazing day out for me. On the return journey I was allowed to sit on the back of the bike. I remember seeing a sign, Leeds 10, and I thought, *This isn't Leeds 10, this is Hunslet*; that's how unworldly I was, because obviously it meant that Leeds was 10 miles away!

We used to play duck stone and beddy, plus British bull dog. During the six-week holidays, we played outside from dawn to dusk. Although we were skint and had nothing, what a wonderful childhood we had.

TV

The first folk in Hunslet to get a telly were Mr and Mrs Booth. Luckily for me, my best friend was Wilfred Booth. At five every evening it was Children's Hour. We absolutely loved it. Wilfred, Jack Priestly and I were glued to it in the Booths' living room. Jack fell out with us for some reason and stopped coming. One afternoon, we were coming out of Low Road School and Jack shouted, "Have you still got that black and white old telly, Willy? We're getting a new one tomorrow and it's colour."

"But you've got all gas in your house, Jack, you've got no electricity," we laughed.

"We're having a cable through the wall," he said, obviously making it up. He'd clearly been missing our hour of TV escapism. We all remained firm friends until Wilfred and Jack disembarked my 'Train of Life' at stops way back.

Low Road School photo. I'm second from the right in the third row up

3. Cupid

Sprinkled with Angel Dust

When I was 14, I was in the 12th and 13th battalion of the parachute regiment army cadets. As we were going up York Road in the back of a lorry, two girls were sat on a gate we passed. Silhouetted by the sun, they waved to the soldiers and I, of course, waved back. My favourite film as a kid was *To Hell and Back* starring Audie Murphy, so I guess that's why I always wanted to be a hero parachutist. Later in life I went to a recruitment office to be in the Marines, but I had a lazy eye, so apparently I wouldn't be able to use a gun!

Two years later, I went to a dance in the Old Mecca, Leeds, with my mates Roy and Keith. It was late September 1962 when the Gaffer Above sprinkled His angel dust on me. I was smitten the moment I spotted the most gorgeous pair of legs, stood at the side of the dance floor. I went up and asked for a dance, but she said, "No, you're drunk." I went a walk round the dance floor and then I approached her again, and took her handbag off her and passed it to Keith. "Don't rifle that bag!" she said.

My mates were teasing, "Passionate Pash has a date!" I was such a good rock and roller, she had to be impressed! She'd just had her 17th birthday, and I told her I was 18. I took her home, and it was the same house and same gate at Seacroft I'd passed by in the lorry two years ago. It turned out she was the angel who had been sat on the gate waving when I was fourteen. That's how my best friend and soul mate, the love of my life, came into my life. That's when I met my treasured girl, Pat. I'm her toy boy, by ten months, as she blessed this world on 14th September 1945.

Roy Orbison, the 'Caruso of Rock', was her favourite singer. Not long after we met, there was a 24-hour dance featuring all the big names, an unbelievable line up! There were the Rolling Stones, the Beatles, Cilla Black, just everyone.

They were giving the audience oxygen to keep them going, no drugs. Pat went with her best mate, Pauline, so I said I'd meet them there later, in order to give myself time to figure how to get in without a ticket! Roy and I found a wooden wall which we could sneak through. We ended up on a toilet seat in the ladies and, of course, who was in there but Pat and Pauline (you couldn't make it up) who ranted, "I told you he was rough." People used to say to Pat, "You're not a match, he's too rough for you," but I'd had an honest upbringing. She stuck with me through thick and thin, my angel, Pat.

First Date with Pat

We went for a coffee – you couldn't get alcohol in the Mecca, except in the Key Hole club upstairs. That didn't last long, she was soon asking for gin and lime, half a crown. What! She's always been an expensive bird! I took her to the bus stop, at the side of the market. The Sonny and Cher song 'I Got You Babe' was out and we used to sing it to each other as we waited for her bus. She wouldn't let me kiss her on that first night, but Passionate Pash invited her to the Wimpy bar on Wednesday. On the next date I thought she'd stood me up, because I couldn't see her. Then Keith shouted out, "She's there in that doorway." She was right shy!

It was three months before I took her home. I missed the last bus. It was teemin' down, cats and dogs. "Ask your mum if I can stay on the sofa," I said.

Her dad, Mr Barnes, shot out, and I thought he'd gone for a blanket, but he returned with a trilby and mackintosh! "It'll save you getting wet when you walk to Leeds!" There were no buses, so I thumbed a lift to Leeds and then got the last bus to Belle Isle. My mam used to say, "You're in love, our Leon."

I'd say, "How do you know that?"

"When you come off that late night bus and I'm in bed, I can hear you running. You're happy, I know you're in love." I was working away in Stoke on Trent when Kennedy got shot. I was working nights with Billy Jeavons, my cousin, steel-fixing. One night, before I went to bed, I wrote Pat a letter, "I'm sorely missing you, and when I get back, I think I've got to talk to you about summat, so how do you think about me putting a ring on your finger?" When I got back, she was over the moon, so I went in to ask Jack for her hand. He said, "It's about bloody time!" Jack and Mary had one son and five girls including Pat. My Pat said she wanted a white wedding, and I said I knew that because she hardly let me touch her, each Wednesday night when we went to the old picture house. We were madly in love. Jack never once paid for a wedding. He wouldn't even come to the wedding so Pat's brother-in-law gave her away.

I got the engagement ring on Briggate from Greenwoods. Pat had spotted the ring she loved, a blue sapphire with diamond chippings in white gold. It cost me £40 which was a hell of a lot then! Sadly, years later she damaged it while bowling, so when we were in Mauritius, I bought five diamonds and took them to a jeweller in Leeds and got her a new ring made. I took the old one for sizing. She never takes it off, so I guess she loved it!

Me

My girl, 6 Kippax Street

My Patricia

Courting days

1962 – Our very first New Year's Eve in the Old Mecca

Our wedding day, 2ⁿᵈ October, 1965

4. Finding a Way

Early Entrepreneur

I've already provided you with a slight insight into my money-making ways, but I was born a grafter, and I'll make a penny wherever I can to provide for my loved ones. I used to go coal picking down the side of the river. Coal waggons would pass and we'd collect any that fell, to sell to our neighbours. Before I left school, I got a butcher's job with Arthur Buller.

"Go to the slaughter house, middle of Leeds, and say you've come for a pig," Arthur instructed! He gave me the heavy metal-framed butcher's bike. When I got there, they gave me a full pig. I tried it in the bike basket. I struggled, but of course it wouldn't fit! I put it across the back of the saddle instead, and I had to push the ginormous weight back at least three miles.

"You're the first one to do it!" Arthur's eyes were wide open! Obviously, a task set to separate the dossers from the grafters!

Another friend, Geoff, had an amazing gift from his parents: a brand-new racing bike. I was in awe of this bike. He joined Meanwood Wheelers, and was off to fabulous places like Scarborough on his bike. I begged Arthur to let me borrow the butcher's bike so I could join the days out.

"Don't be bloody silly, you won't get out of Leeds, never mind Scarborough!" Arthur jeered. "Take it, and I'll give your mam free meat for a week if you make it!"

I took the basket off to make it lighter. I'm made of determined stuff, so of course I made it, but I was absolutely shattered and the laugh of the trip! I just had no energy to pedal back, but I wanted that meat for my mam so I devised a little plan. I let my tyres down and thumbed a lift, and the Gaffer Above sent a lovely white van which took me and the bike all the way home, while Geoff and his posh cycle pedalled home!

After that I saved money from my butcher's job and newspaper round to buy a Freddie Grubb bike. It cost 40 quid and it was well worth it. From then on, me and my bike went everywhere with Meanwood Wheelers.

The World of Work

I haven't got a piece of paper to my name, no qualifications at all, but I've got on in life through common sense and hard work! My school used to send us on factory tours, but nothing in that world appealed to me whatsoever, so I ended up in Middleton Pit. I loved it at first. I was there 18 months, but I didn't want to be a pony driver anymore, and the pits were closing down. I worked in the saw mill. It built my body up, using the saw. Trevor worked there and we got on great. I was his lad, and my job was to pull the planks through so his hand wouldn't slip and chop his fingers off! He took me out in his mini, and taught me to drive. Some great lads worked at the pit. The brickie, Alan Price, left some great pieces of art in his brickwork there when it closed.

I gave my notice in and went onto building sites, but then the depression hit. I became a jack-of all-trades, window cleaning while holding down a job at the copper works. There were three different shifts. I needed the money for the mortgage, which went up every month with interest rates. It was scandalous. People used to laugh at me, working all those hours, and say, "Come out on the dole," but that wasn't my way. I had to work for my living.

Settling Down

A day from heaven: noon, 2nd October 1965, three years after we met, my Pat became my wife. We paid for the white wedding ourselves. We didn't scrimp. We had a choir. Susan, Pat's sister, was a bridesmaid, my brother Roy was a page boy, and of course there was dancing in the evening for my dancing queen. We happily settled down in our tiny, back-to-back terrace with its toilet down the street. We couldn't afford a honeymoon, but I saved like mad for my Pat and flew her off to Majorca 12 months later. We were so excited, as it was the first time either of us had been on a plane.

We were blessed with the arrival of our two Parrish princes, Quinn and Marcus, whilst residing in our tiny terrace. Quinn gave us a shock as he ended up in hospital during his first three months, short of calcium and very poorly. Thankfully, the Gaffer Above looked after him for us and he pulled through; he's now six foot two! Quinn's name came from Quinn Martin Productions off the telly. Some of his friends have babies named after him! Marcus Lee completed our family a year and ten months after Quinn. I am so proud to be the dad of two lads. I think the boss upstairs knew better than to give me a daughter; I'd have been much too overprotective! Marcus has given us our grandson. Macaulay was our Christmas angel, born on December 17th 1994.

We loved it in our first nest, all the kids playing out in the street. We were happy with our lot – our tin bath, our tiny two-bedroomed house was our palace. Everyone could leave their doors open on Kippax Street Leeds 9, the best place ever, just over the road from Hampton pub! Patricia was a trained tailor, but she stopped at home and looked after the kids. She used to bring clothes home for them which her tailor mates had made a mess of on purpose! Nobody had any money for new clothes in those days.

My Pat sometimes lost her temper with me. She is the boss! My cousin, Billy, lived behind us in his back-to-back, so when I wanted to go for a pint I'd bang on the wall and he'd bang back. I'd say to the wife, "I'm off to the pub." Once I had gone to the toilet, which was down the street. I tried to get into Billy's house because he was having a party! When I came back home, Pat had the metal bin lid and hit me with it like a scene from Tom and Jerry. She was pregnant with Quinn at the time, so it must have been her hormones!

Continual Battle to Make Ends Meet

Later on, I started taxi driving. I'm your original handyman because I'll try any job to clothe and feed my family. I worked for Streamline at Christmas, and I put a Santa Claus outfit on as I'll always try to put a smile on people's faces.

The office complained because everyone was ringing up saying they wanted Santa Claus to drive them!

I lived at Rothwell and a young girl, in Leeds city centre, wanted a cab to Pudsey at half one in the morning! When I dropped her off, she said, "I'll just go to my house and get my money!" So, I watched her run up a little alley and I suddenly twigged. She'd done a runner and owed me about six quid! I rang head office and they said not to worry, because they'd just taken a call from Pudsey for someone wanting a lift. So, I took the call and this lad and lass got in. They asked me to leave them alone for a quick talk and they'd pay me 15 pounds! I gave them 20 minutes – of course, I kept the key. When I returned, he said he was off, but asked me to take her home. So, I asked for payment: 25 quid to Rothwell. As I lived there, it was looking like the Gaffer Above was sorting out my night's earnings! When I pulled up at the house, a man came out and gave the lass a love. It was only her husband, thanking me for bringing his wife home! "How much do I owe you?" was music to my ears. Her face was a picture when I charged him £25. She couldn't say anything! I'd been surrounded by angels, again, and I was able to go home and provide for my own family.

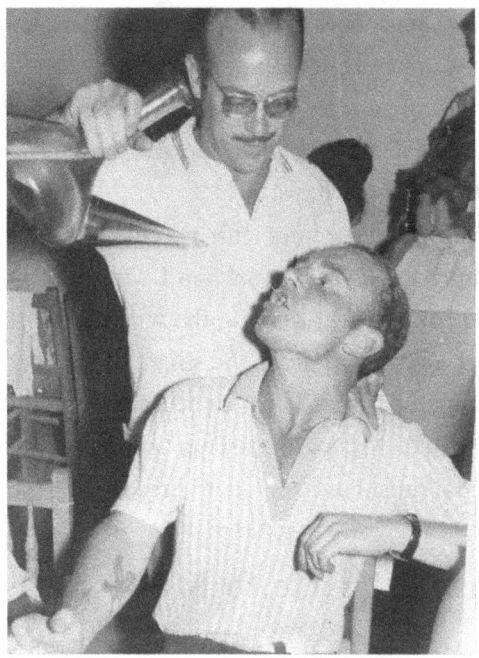

on 1st holiday abroad 1966

Quinn

Quinn and Marcus

Karen, Quinn and Patricia

5. Dreams Become Reality

Things Start to Get Better

I met Peter Babington on a building site; I was a steel fixer, he was a joiner. He had a scrap yard in Middleton, which he was struggling with. He asked me if I wanted to go into business with him, but I was honest and said, "I don't know anything about it, mate. I'm happy doing what I'm doing." He insisted he could do with someone coming in, would I take a look? So, I visited his yard at Cross Green. I thought, "This could actually be a good business." I asked him what he wanted in order for me to join. His requirement of four thousand pounds was a lot of money in 1975, so I had to go to a bank to borrow it. After 18 months I went up and asked him what was happening, because I'd not seen much advancement on my investment. We came to an agreement that I would buy him and the other two lads out. I became a workaholic.

I was determined I was going to make a success of that business, and in 1977 it was all mine!

I was prepared to defend that yard with my life. I do have waggon-loads of people management skills, so I found a way of befriending the gipsies after a few minor conflicts. We became good pals, the kids waving as they passed the yard. I had a driver working for me, and someone tipped me off that he was sleeping in lay-bys on the job! So, I put a tracker on him, and when I found him asleep, I crept up and pinched his key as he slumbered on. I had a great laugh when I sat in my car behind and rang his phone! I saw him jump out of his skin, and I heard him lie through his teeth when he answered my call, not knowing I was behind him. I told him to get a move on, and I couldn't stop my laughter as I saw him looking everywhere for his key. Of course, after that, he never messed me around again. I nicknamed him Jim Speed, because he was so slow, and I even put that name on a truck for a while, as a laugh! I had quite a reputation, I know that, because when I first took him on, people said, "That boss is a lunatic, you don't want to work for him." But he was still with me years later, so I can't have been that bad!

Babington's, My Baby

My yard is called Babington's after its first owner, Babbis for short. It's well known, so although I considered changing the name to "Parrish and Sons" There never seemed to be a good reason because everyone knew us for what we were. I bought Peter out over five years and every month, without fail, my payment went through. At the end of the five years, I celebrated my last payment. He came over, all beaming, praising me for never having missed his fee. He said he was off to Spain to celebrate his new freedom.

My solicitor had put a clause in the agreement, preventing Peter from opening a yard within so many miles for five years. Apparently, it's sort of standard practise, but Peter asked for it to be taken out, as he would want to train his son up sometime. Being good friends, I obliged. Then one Thursday, I was reading the paper and my eyes nearly popped out of my head! I read that he'd put in for planning for a yard near ours.

I was bouncing! I was absolutely bouncing! Not with joy, I can tell you. I went round and kicked in all the walls in that his brickie was laying. I grabbed the son by the throat and told him this place wasn't Babington Car Spares – my place was. I ordered him to take his sign off the wall, and I smashed his office up. I told him to get his dad to ring me when I got back.

Within the week, one of our regular customers said he'd been to our other yard, Babington's, down Hunslet! I went down, pulled all the phones out and turfed two of them out of the office in pure anger. He was living off the name I'd purchased over five years of payment, and he was telling customers that it was my second yard! I went up in my old Sherpa pickup. The gate was padlocked. Peter was there with his son and another guy. They told me I wasn't going in or they'd call the police! I told Peter he'd screwed me over, that of all people I didn't expect it from him. They threw bricks at me, so I picked an axe up and I smashed the lock off the gates! I'd cracked up and, in my temper, I smashed in the big thick oak door and went into kitchen. Then they called the police, but I wasn't bothered because they were the crooks. I couldn't get through the second door, so I wrecked the kitchen instead.

I went home and I told Pat that the police would be coming soon. I explained everything to her, and she thought I'd done right. My Pat will always support me. Within 15 minutes the police came, dogs, vans and all, to pick up the mad axe man. Seeing me so calm, the officer sent the rest of the police away. I knew it would probably go to court and thought, "What have I let myself in for with my bloody temper?"

Anyway, Peter saw sense and decided not to press charges. He stopped his yard and sold the land for a roundabout, so he did alright out of it. Sadly, Peter got cancer and Alzheimer's, so I bit the bullet and went up to see him; after all, once a mate, always a mate. I shook his hand and we made up, and we both agreed that we were all a bit mad in those days! The whole incident shows, though, how Babington Car Spares is very dear to me and, just as I would for my family, I'll do anything in my power to protect the yard.

6. A Mountain to Climb

Help, I Need the Gaffer Above

When I was about 35, I got stomach cancer. I took all sorts of remedies. Aged 42 I almost died but somehow, with help from the Gaffer, I survived. It wasn't an easy ride. At 50 I went through another bad time – I honestly didn't think I was going to make 51. 1999 was such a bad year. My mam died from a heart attack, aged 82, in an ambulance outside her house. I sorted her funeral for her. That tore me apart. I was so close to her. It was, without doubt, the worst time of my life.

Mam used to play the piano in local pubs for pin money. She played by ear: she'd just ask people to hum and then she'd play what they'd hummed. She couldn't read music. None of her children were musical. I can just about play 'Here We Go Round the Mulberry Bush' with one finger! I never told my mam I was ill. I had to go to Pinderfields hospital not long after she died. I knew it was bad news when the doctor told me to take a seat. He told me 'It' was serious, and if I didn't have the operation, I'd only have 10 months to live. It was a Thursday, and he instructed me to go into hospital on the Tuesday. I sat in the car park wondering how I could tell Pat.

Some friends had already booked for us to go to Cuba with them so I decided, you only live once, so we went on holiday and I never told Pat about my 10-month death sentence! On the plane journey back home, I thought perhaps I should tell her. She broke down in the toilet and called me every name under the sun. Quinn picked us up from the airport, and he told us that the hospital had been phoning every day wanting to speak to me. So, I went straight in for the operation. My lads carried on working at the yard. I could trust them completely. The actual cancer operation was a complete success, and I came round and all my stomach was stapled up. Job done, we all believed.

Deteriorating Fast

The wife came to see me after the operation, and we thought I'd be up and about and back to normal in no time, but a couple of days after that I started to deteriorate fast. The last thing I remember is the doctor looking into my wound before I went into a coma of some sort. Apparently, during major operation, the doctor had nicked my bowels. They took me down, opened me up and realised I was dying of peritonitis. I had no idea of this, lost in my coma. The wound was left open as they didn't expect me to survive, because no one survives stomach cancer followed by such severe peritonitis. I survived both! The Gaffer Upstairs sent me back. He wasn't ready for me!

Comatose

I was in a coma for three months. My wife was coming in, talking to me. She knew all the nurses in intensive care. I meanwhile knew none of this! I do remember coming out of the coma. I was lying on a piece of wood. It was absolutely pitch black, and I couldn't see or hear a thing. However, somehow, I was aware of three people on my right.

Waterfalls

I thought, hang on a minute, we're on water. I couldn't hear the water but I knew we were floating on it, on our boards. I thought, what the hell's happening here? And I sensed that further down there was a waterfall. "I've gotta get off this. I'm not going over the waterfalls," I said to myself, but the more I tried to get off the board the more I realised that I couldn't move. Just at that very moment, right before I was about to go over the waterfall, there was a huge crack on my left. Lightening seemed to follow the crack, which woke me up. Somehow it gave me the strength to get off the board.

I looked at the door and turned round and it was completely black. When I looked round to where I'd come from, the other three people were going over the waterfall. I knew that they were, but I couldn't see them. I saw the door, all hazy, so I put my hand through it, and I was feeling my Pat's face.

I'd bought her a crucifix, years ago, so I grabbed it from round her neck and that's when I opened my eyes. The nurses had come running as she couldn't get my hand off the crucifix. They took the chain off so I could hold it. Then I fell back unconscious for another week.

When I did come round, I told the doctor the tale and he said, "You know, Leon, in this job nothing surprises me anymore." He said there had been three patients in the beds on my right, and within the last week they'd all died! I think God sent me back down for a reason, and I'm still trying to find out what the reason is.

Seeing My Stomach

As I got a bit of my strength back, I begged to be allowed into the toilet to swill water over my head, as I wasn't allowed a bath. They put me in a wheelchair and pushed me in. I can't explain to you how amazing the feeling of splashing water over my head was. Then I looked in the mirror, and I couldn't believe my eyes when a little withered old man stared back at me! I looked over my shoulder to see if it was someone else, but no, – it was me. At that point I looked down at my stomach, which I'd lifted the bandages from. I screamed. I saw what looked like a baby's head coming out of my belly. I walked and crawled to the door, locked it, screamed and smashed the mirror

Support from Pat

The nurses were hammering on the door but I wouldn't open it. "What's this? What have they done to me?" I screamed. I just went potty. Eventually I agreed to just let Pat in. She started screaming when I showed her. We somehow calmed each other down. When I had been in the coma my stomach muscles had wasted away. Pat is an angel in disguise. She always has been throughout our marriage, but especially during my hospital stay. After my operation in Pinderfields, I got deep vein thrombosis. It swells up when I travel, so I have to put flight socks on.

Home from Hospital

They sent me home, but I was still very weak. My grandson Macaulay was very young, and I'd sit out in the garden with him. When I came home and saw the garden, for the first time, I cried. Pat had done the garden, made it beautiful for me to sit in. There was a little pond with three steps to it. I'll never forget Macaulay holding my hand to help me walk them. Physically he was more of a hindrance than a help, bless him, but emotionally that lad helped heal me.

I was left by that hospital to endure almost five years of unbearable pain and mental stress, with my stomach literally hanging out in a sack of skin! I started putting weight on. I couldn't get up because I had no stomach muscles – Pat had to pull me up. In the end we got a kitchen chair for me to hold on to, to pull myself up. My stomach bulged out when I stood up. As time went on, I looked pregnant – my intestines, everything, was hanging out. Pat bought two old roll on corsets and cut the suspenders off. She got one for the top and one for the bottom of my stomach. It was a huge help! I got referred to St James's by a fantastic doctor, but they still did nothing to mend my stomach as they didn't know what to do. It was a terrible mess, unbearable really.

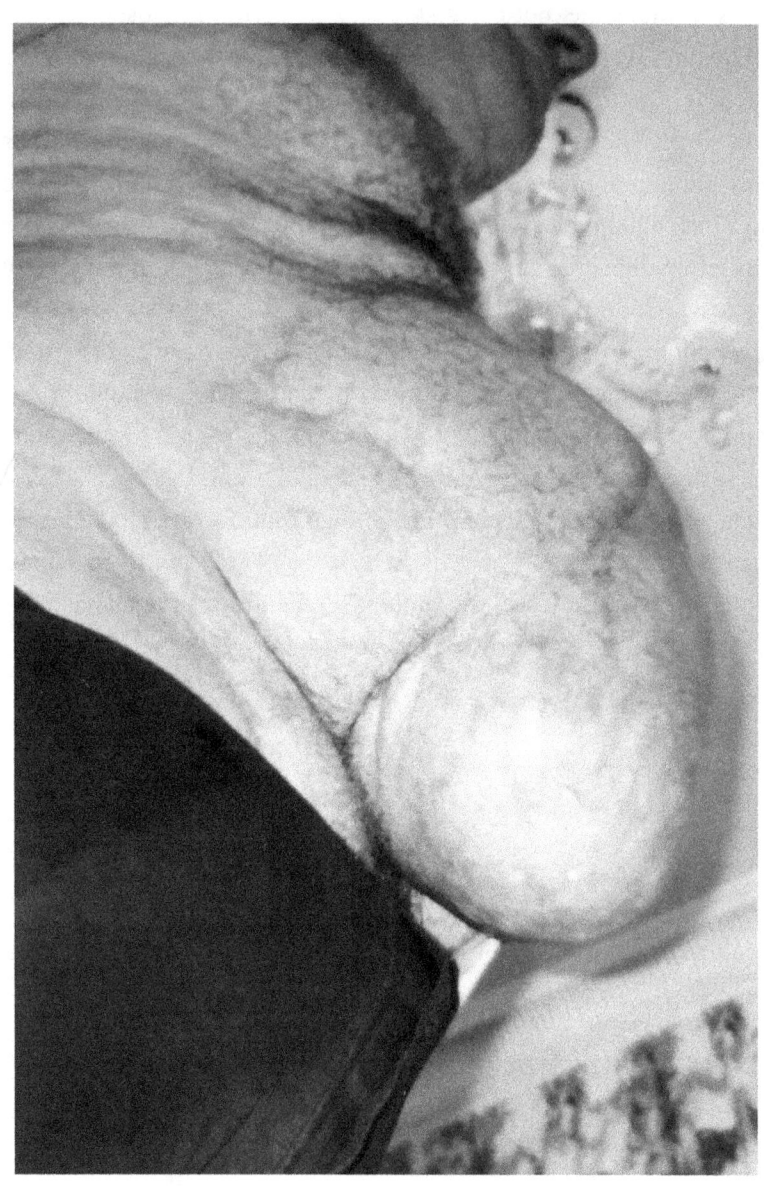

Five and a half years in excruciating pain

7. Guardians

Amazing American Angels

A friend gave me the details of an American hospital which dealt with the war wounded. I chose to go in September, and took Pat with me. I also took Quinn, so he could look after her until the op was over, because it was going to be a big operation, and I feared that I might not make it home. I had no insurance for the flight so I just made a number up on the phone. I said to the wife and Quinn, "If anything happens to me over there, don't go to the expense of burying me, just bring me back in a box and put my remains next to me mam in Hunslet."

After we'd arrived, we were walking to a new hotel, because the one we had hoped to stay in was fully booked. Outside the new hotel there were two 20-foot angel wings, magnificent, and I took it as a sign that the Gaffer's angels were going to be looking after me!

American Operation

My organs had adhered to some skin, so it took four and a half hours just to get the skin off, to put my stomach back as it should be. They used skin from the back of a dead guy. I didn't want to know anything about the history of the dead guy, but I had a joke with the surgeons that because I'm ginger, I didn't want skin from a black guy! It just wouldn't go!

They fitted six sheets of mesh to give me some sort of structure. I came round and Pat was there. When she saw my stomach she cried, which made me panic, but she said, "No Leon, it's absolutely marvellous," as more tears streamed down her face. God, the love this girl had for me. She truly is my earth angel.

I sued the NHS, and I won the case so others will benefit. My sufferings helped others not to suffer. I settled for £125,000 but the operation in America had cost over £160,000. I'd also had to repay £35,000 of sick money, paid to me when I had been too ill to work. When I got a bit better, I gave a letter from the American surgeons to my doctor. They'd been appalled that I'd been left like this for five and a half years. The letter explained the treatment I'd received, how they'd performed the operation. I asked my doctors to put it in my file in case I needed further treatment but the letters kept disappearing, all six replacements vanished into thin air!

Additional Angel Anecdotes

As you've probably noticed, I like to treat my girl to a holiday before hospital stays, so I had taken her to Lanzarote for a holiday four weeks previously, before the 'biggie' in America. I wasn't going to be miserable, so we lived up to our usual partying reputation. We were enjoying rock and roll dancing in the hotel when I noticed a man walking directly towards me. Straight out of the blue, with no introduction he said, "Hi Leon, you're going to America for a major operation, and I've been told to find you and talk to you. I knew it was you from the moment I walked through the door because you are surrounded by light and angels." I stared at him, gobsmacked, as he continued, "Angels will look after you, and your mam is watching over you. I know your mam's passed, but she's sent me to give you a message to tell you: she's annoyed you never told her how bad you were, but not to worry as she'll be looking after you this time!"

Then the guy turned and walked out, and to this day I've not a clue who he was. After an experience like that you don't ever feel alone and you feel more aware of things, so it was no surprise when we were being driven home from the airport and saw that the dashboard of the taxi was covered in angels!

Angel wings in Baltimore

8. Looking Up

Paying the Gaffer Back

I started to think, *what am I doing here?* I'd clearly had some miraculous moments. I felt it was time to share some of the care I'd received with others. "I'm going to help in the hospital," I announced to Pat. St James's had a new cancer wing. People would come out crying. When you've been through what I've been through, you get a feeling. I know just by looking at a person if they're suffering. The time had come for me to use this newfound gift to help others.

They gave me a role to be a listening ear, and provide a cuppa when patients had received bad news. I remember one particular girl came in crying and I said, "You can't go back out there looking like that! Come in for a cup of tea, I guess you've had some bad news."

She said, "Yes, I'm terminal, they've given me two years."

I said, "Well that is terminal. I haven't got a whiskey to give you," and she smiled and said she wished I had, but she'd accepted the diagnosis and that's not what was upsetting her! "So," I said, "Well, what is?"

And she replied, "The bloody doctor!"

I said, "Doctors are doctors, they do a marvellous job but they don't know how to talk to people, and that's my job, my little love." She told me I was doing a good job, so I asked her what exactly the doc had said to upset her. She said he'd told her to stop smoking! I asked her if she had any fags on her and she said yes so, I said, "Come outside with me and we'll have a fag in the smoking shelter." I'd stopped smoking by then, but I had one for her! She was so happy, puffing away, and I said, "I'm no doctor, but if I was, I'd tell you to carry on, and now it's up to you!"

She was smiling away as she said, "Well I am going to, as it's the one thing that makes me happy."

I met some marvellous brave people in my hospital volunteer role. It got a bit embarrassing because people were queuing up to see me. One guy I met was called Maurice. He came from Barnsley, and he had cancer in a very bad way. We got on immediately as he was an ex-collier. I put him right. I befriended him. We had plenty of laughs to momentarily forget his plight. There were even longer queues of 10 or 11 people once Maurice had told people to come and see me. He was a right character, and one of the reasons I stopped my hospital volunteer work after four years.

When he found out I was cruising the Caribbean at Christmas he asked me to get him a St Martin t-shirt, so I promised I would. I got back and I'd missed Maurice by three days, he'd gone up to the Gaffer. I was gutted, and I just couldn't carry on. That's when I realised that I was too emotionally involved. I found out when his funeral was, and I thought I'd pop the t-shirt on his coffin but his wife asked for it to wear in bed.

"We want to know what you're saying to the patients," the volunteer office told me. I was a bit shocked, had I done something wrong? They said, no, not at all, in fact the opposite! They showed me a filing cabinet of letters from patients who'd written in praising me, hundreds of letters, but they wouldn't let me read them! They told me they had two trainee counsellors, and that they'd like them to shadow me for a few weeks to learn how to relate so well to the patients. Of course, I let them, but at the end of the day, I had the advantage over them as I'd been down that road myself, and my empathy was natural and sincere.

Treat Others How You'd like Them to Treat You

Right from the start, I decided that my yard was going to treat folk fairly. Therefore, at Babington Car Spares I decided end of life vehicles can be collected and recycled free of charge. We've never charged, and with scrap prices as high as they are, how could we? The people who come to breakers aren't millionaires, and it's not right to charge single mums and pensioners when we can make so much from recycling the vehicles.

Our yard is far removed from the guard-dog-on-a-chain yards. The EVL Directive required us to invest several thousand into specialised equipment, and it's all added to the friendly face of our industry. The myth that recycling yards are the backstop to criminal activity has no place in our business. Our customers include young single mums, old age pensioners, and people who might normally have felt uncomfortable coming to a breakers yard.

I Don't Want to Live in a World Where We Don't Look Out for Each Other

Cars flipped upside down, people trapped inside, a double decker bus, lorries, a nightmare pile up. A full-scale rescue operation was in process. One of the cars burst into flames as the emergency services tried to rescue folk and make the other vehicles safe. Horrific – but thankfully this was just a practise for a real-life situation. I was more than happy to provide the vehicles for the exercise, which hopefully will ensure real lives are saved in future. I also donated a scrap car to help fire-fighters at Garforth in their training. The Nissan Bluebird stands outside the station to be used by fire-fighters to practise their extraction skills. We all hope there are few real-life scenarios where they do have to cut people free, but my little blue car will hopefully have enabled one life to have been saved somewhere. Fire-fighters were always welcome to visit my yard to practise their skills. During the fire-fighters' strike, my yard became the temporary training ground for Green Goddess crews who were shown car cutting techniques by an RAF breathing and rescue team. If there's ever an opportunity to help out, I'm up for it.

If You Ever Need a Helping Hand, You'll Find One at the End of Your Arm

For some reason, I was born with lots of get up and go. 'Where there's a will, there's a way' is probably another of my mottos for life. I will persevere. I will find the solution to the problem, and one of the best solutions in my life has been to help others despite my own problems. Having said that, I do believe people have to help themselves too, and as my story has shown I have always been a hard grafter, often holding down several jobs at once in order to make ends meet. There's no place for scroungers in my world. Society doesn't owe anyone a living. Nothing comes to anyone who sits on their rump all day. Having pride in yourself is the first rung of the ladder. Often my own problems have enabled me to have more empathy for the plight of others.

St Gemma's Hospice in Moortown, Leeds holds a special place in my heart, and it was with great pleasure that my LMD Parrish trust was able to replace the old hospital style beds with new profiling beds. Unable to join the Yorkshire Cancer Centre Great Wall of China trek, due to my medical issues, I threw myself into fundraising to send Sandra and Daz (Sandaz). I raised £3,000 in a fantastic evening at the Hunslet Club for Boys. I organised a raffle, an auction, Irish dancing and a Frank Sinatra tribute singer. I will always think of some attraction to draw the crowds in order to raise funds for a charity, which has found a place in my heart. Sandra sadly lost both her parents within nine months of each other to cancer. They both died at St James's, so the money Sandaz raised, £11,000 on this occasion, bought two special machines for the hospital.

Having suffered from cancer myself, I will do all I can, everything in my power, to help other sufferers. What better prize for a raffle to support Yorkshire Cancer Centre than two footballs signed by the Leeds team which knocked Manchester united out of the FA cup? So, I sorted those for an event at Rothwell Working Men's Club, raising £2,000 for new equipment, medical research and home-from-home comforts for patients. I always say that if you're going to have a bit of a do, then it's got to be done properly, so Patrick Kisnorbo kindly agreed to pull out the winning tickets. Singer Jason Guest compered the evening, and the band True Brit performed.

I try to think outside the box and find a unique way to support charities. For example, I responded to the mayoral appeal, Candlelighters, with a donation raised from selling some Sean Connery look-a-like photographs. Macmillan Cancer Support are ace, so it was much appreciated when Yorkshire cricket captain, Andrew Gale, took players Joe Sayers and Steve Patterson to the Robert Ogden Macmillan centre at St James's hospital, where I volunteered. The visit launched Macmillan Cancer Support's status as partner of Yorkshire cricket club. I was chuffed when Andrew gave me a cricket hat.

I was honoured when the Yorkshire Evening Post ran an article which described me as one of the city's most colourful charity stalwarts. I raised over £250,000 in the 30 years I spent organising fundraising events. Decades of fun events included a bikini beach party at a local golf club in the middle of winter, and a Christmas party in the middle of summer! The beach party enabled us to provide lots of games and goodies for the children's ward at St James's. They received five colour TVs and radios, craft items, videos and cassettes. I've been heavily involved with the kids' wards at Jimmy's, and it broke my heart to see the sick kids in there. One Christmas I visited the wards dressed as Santa. My wig fell off. I'm completely bald, and one of the kids who was having chemo was delighted – he said, "See, Santa's bald just like us!" It's moments like that which made all my charity work worthwhile. I find it really heart-warming when everybody pulls together.

I'll do anything for my mates, and I decided to organise a close shave for a Selby Colliery worker, Steven Clark, who was paralysed in a rugby accident. I arranged for six of us to shave our heads to support him. I'm bald, so I wanted to organise a Leon lookalike contest to raise money. We raised £1,000. In total £30,000 was raised for Steven.

My finale was at the Hunslet Club when I raised £3,000 for the Robert Ogden Macmillan Centre at St James's Hospital, Leeds. We auctioned a painting by notorious prisoner, Charles Bronson. In all my time of doing charity work, one guy always came along to help, however busy he was. He would pick out the winning raffle tickets, talk to the guests, whatever. He is the legendary footballer, Leeds United striker Peter 'Lash' Lorimer, or '90 miles an hour'. He once had a shot of his recorded at that speed! I can never thank Peter enough, and we are firm friends to this day!

Stretching a Promise

If I promise something, I'll keep it. In a moment of madness, I promised my friends that I would take them to the motor show in a stretch limousine if I won the lottery. So, despite winning just a tenner, I hired a white 32-foot 10-seater super stretch for six mates plus one of my sons.

Me and Leeds United number 7, Peter Lorimer – friends for ever

Me in Sun City, singing into the original Elvis Presley microphone

9. Supporter

If You Were Born with the Ability to Change Someone's Perspective, Use It

If I think I have the ability to influence somebody in a position of power with a letter, I'll write it. Anything that I feel is unjust, I'll try to make just by voicing my opinion. For example, I wrote to the press about fuel prices. I included suggestions, and I value the readers who respond.

The Rt Hon. William Hague was the recipient of my letter to suggest the establishment of an NHS lottery. On another issue, Gordon Brown replied with a great postcard of his residence, Number 10! The Prince of Wales said he was grateful for me, taking the trouble to send him a video about royalty and a federal Europe. The Speaker's Office replied swiftly to my letters, as did Peter Lilley when he was Shadow Chancellor. Prime Minister Blair passed my letter on to the Department of Environment, Transport and the Regions.

As Martin Luther King pointed out, our lives begin to end when we choose to be silent on the things that matter; so if I have a view on something, I'll give it, and why not use the media to voice my opinion? Therefore, I wrote to the newspapers about the plans to charge motorists to drive into Leeds city centre. It had been estimated that £130,000 a day would be collected from motorists driving into Leeds. I was initially against the idea but then I pointed out it could be a good idea if each time the motorist paid the fee, they would receive share options in the new transport system! The big stores would pull out of the centre because, in reality, people like myself wouldn't pay the fees, so the centre would probably just end up one big housing estate.

Likewise, I wrote to my local paper concerning the North-South divide in Leeds cemeteries. I felt it was unacceptable that bereaved families in south Leeds faced an obstacle course of ditches, litter and rubbish when visiting their loved ones at Hunslet Cemetery. It was terribly neglected. The only water tap was broken, so grave flowers couldn't be kept in bloom. It especially upset me when I was at the cemetery for my dear mam's burial. Disabled people wouldn't have been able to access the cemetery due to the ditches, and it was disrespectful that a huge pile of soil was being used as a BMX hill. In contrast, the cemetery at Lawnswood, across the city, was in magnificent condition.

Either I'll find a way, or I'll make one concerning any matter that bothers me. Therefore, I decided to take matters into my own hands and improve the cemetery for Mam, myself. My lasting memorial to my marvellous mam will be mighty oaks for my mighty mam. On the day of her funeral, I collected acorns from Hunslet cemetery. I cared for them and grew them into saplings. Then I planted five of them around the cemetery. Don't worry, I like to do things by the book, and I got permission from Leeds City Council and their park division. In addition, I spoke out, via the newspaper, to appeal to folk to stop nicking the wind chimes from the cemetery. My mam loved a tune, and that's why we kept placing the wind chimes there.

I voiced my concern to the press for the plight of thousands of Leeds people left without a dentist as surgeries rushed to privatise the practises. Our beliefs make us who we are, and I believe in standing for what is right even if it means standing alone. So, my letters to the press to try and help society continued, and I wrote about chemicals which are killing us on our foods. In a nutshell my message was: Let's stop all the chemical spraying now, but please let's have our organic foods at the right price.

Having been in hospital so many times and for so long, a cause that is very important to me is, of course, the NHS. I feel that matron should return! Just by being there in the wards, the nurses would know who to turn to when the unexpected happens. I feel this would relieve the nurses of the extra burden of ward management. The plight of patients in hospital obviously means a lot to me so I was very upset to hear about the cushy life in prison. So yes, another letter to the press. I couldn't stand to think of the prisoners I had read about in Armley prison having cups of tea on demand and colour televisions, while hospital patients have to pay a daily rate for the privilege of a TV.

I'm somebody who values the local community, so I decided to explain, once again to the press that, for local folk longstanding street names are important. They hold cherished memories. I didn't feel that our planners had taken into account the feelings of local residents. Hunslet folk have lost familiar landmarks including the Anchor Inn. I wrote to plead for the name 'Anchor Street' to be given back to us in place of the name 'The Oval'.

I will also speak up for protecting our environment. The papers received yet another letter from me concerning Tulip Street in Hunslet. Workmen had stripped the street of thirty mature trees. Lots of people were devastated by this loss, but you need to shout out about it and that's where I will always go a step further. I was convinced that if the trees were in Alwoodley they wouldn't have been touched. I wish more people would speak up in times like this, and then we might all get answers and win the fight, that many just moan about quietly.

When poll tax was a thing, I stuck up for the honest citizen of Leeds by writing to the paper to try and stop the 15% rise. I often had replies printed to my letters so folk do take notice. You should give it a go!

Leon's Lot of Bottle

If I'm not writing to the press or the House of Commons or even the Queen, I'll still have plenty to say! *How about a message in a bottle*, I thought, while sailing in the middle of the Atlantic Ocean. I wrote a note on the back of a postcard and placed it in a plastic bottle, along with a five dollar note for the postage. Two years later, I received a phone call from Guadeloupe – how good was that! Lucky Leon became my official nickname after that, because I threw that bottle in the sea while on the journey of hope; when I was going to America for that life-saving surgery I told you about.

Leeds United: Wear Your Shirt with Pride

As a devoted Leeds United fan, I was determined to make the journey to Prague to cheer on the Elland Roaders, despite my recent cancer surgery. I had previously travelled to watch my team in Rome, and a friend had prepared a document in Italian to show the Carabinieri so they would treat me gently when they carried out searches on Leeds fans. Leeds University were brilliant, and they provided a language expert to write a note for my Prague trip, so I was off to support Leeds abroad, yet again.

The Leeds game in Milan found supporter Proud Parrish present again, cheering them on to triumph. We loved the match, but not that much that we wanted to get stranded! Our muttonhead Milanese coach driver got lost, and so we missed the plane home. A few of us managed to pay for another flight, but guess what, the baggage got lost!

I was there supporting them in Istanbul at the Beşiktaş game. Thankfully, due to ill health at the time, I couldn't go to the Galatasaray game where two of our supporters were sadly murdered. So many matches come to mind; for example, I enjoyed the match when we beat Liverpool 4-3, and Mark Viduka scored all four and lifted every supporter's spirits up.

When I sponsored Hunslet Boys' Club, we had sportsman's dinner, and who should come along but Billy Bremner and Norman Hunter? That is a special photo. I had a season ticket, which I stopped when some matches were terrible; we were leaving matches at half time and finishing watching in the pub! I used to sit in the old cop, then the West stand but the atmosphere wasn't as good as the cop.

I loved watching Macaulay play as much as I did Leeds United, and I nearly burst with pride when he used to win man of the match, for example while playing for the Durker Devils.

Rugby League

I went to watch Leeds Rhinos at Wembley. We lost to Wigan, but we always make our days out, a time to remember; the performance of *Lion King* didn't let Pat down, but I was bored! I had a go at tight fisted Leeds RL fans who kept their hands in their pockets during a collection I had raised for a baby scanner. After a Leeds vs. Bradford match, hundreds of fans walked past the collectors. A children's rugby team had laid a world record 1,290 ft. woollen scarf, knit in Leeds RL club's blue, amber and white, around the pitch at half time. They'd hoped to raise £1000 but only got £150 from the crowd of over 11,000. As a sponsor of the Hunslet boys' rugby team I had earlier carried the scarf around the streets of Rothwell.

From left to right: Leeds United number 6, Norman Hunter, me, and Leeds United Captain, Fantastic number 4, Billy Bremner

10. Busy Business

Trouble at the Yard

I built a furnace at the yard, and one day I was working on it, ladling aluminium out of the back of the furnace, which is a pretty dangerous job. You have to really concentrate on it, so I was rather distracted when a policeman, who liked to come in to chat, came along. Lots of police popped in for a cup of tea. We had nothing to hide, it was the best-run yard in England.

"Is it alright if I use your phone, Leon, as my wife's about to have a baby?" I told him to feel free to use my office. So, he went in and as I looked around, I saw him driving off, and you know how you get a gut feeling in your stomach? I thought, *something's not right there.* There was a thousand pounds missing in ten-pound notes. I knew immediately because I always kept a two thousand float, and even if I didn't earn enough to get the lads' wages, I still wouldn't touch it in case a machine or a pick-up broke down and I needed cash. I tried ringing the policeman but he wouldn't answer, so I phoned the police which was obviously a tricky thing to do, ringing the police to complain about one of their own. Within twenty minutes my yard was covered in police. A Detective Inspector suggested gipsies, but I knew who it was without a doubt. The police searched the yard and couldn't find it. I told them the suspect was doing up an old car. They found the car and did a thorough search and found my money, stuffed under the carpet, under the pedals.

All hell broke loose as none of them wanted to believe their own man would do such a thing – after all, everyone hates a bent copper.

"Do you know who he is?" they asked me, "He's the son of the Chief of West Yorkshire police."

It didn't bother me who he was, I wanted justice. Two weeks down the line I was still pushing for charges when I got a phone call from a very posh lady, "Do you realise what you're doing to a very nice man, ruining his career? You've got two sons yourself; well, we'll be watching you!" I went straight to the police but I had no evidence of the phone call. The Detective Inspector told me that because he was pursuing charges on my behalf, his police career would go no further, and sadly he never did get promotion.

The bent copper got three months inside. Life should have carried on as normal in the yard after that, but we knew there was a grudge against us. We got three raids by police, one at three in the morning, and one at six in the morning at my home! We got a raid at the yard claiming that 16 of our cars were stolen property. Even though we explained that they can't have been, because they were all registered there in the book with their details, they sent someone in to take those sixteen cars to the police compound. We never did get them back!

They arrested me and my two sons. Our solicitor came down, but we ended up in the Crown Court behind petitions. It was a very frightening experience, I can tell you, when we were ordered to take our shoes off, remove our belts. We realised how serious this accusation was as we looked at the Brief through the glass. We were in despair, but he sort of smiled with his hands up and we thought, "Hold on, there's nothing to smile about, mate!" As procedures commenced the judge stood up. There was a stranger in the gallery opposite who waved his hand and walked off. Suddenly the judge said there was no case to answer for! All trumped-up charges.

We considered suing the police so we hired a solicitor in Manchester. We soon discovered that nobody wants to take a police chief to court. Inspector Ronnie Johnson restored our confidence in the police, however. He told us that he knew we were straight. We became firm friends, and he even invited us to his retirement party. He gave us a lot of business with old cars from his division which had to be dismantled and given to scrap. Ronnie also restored our self-belief. My yard is the straightest yard in Britain. I refused to do false insurance claims or to be bent. I've got a good rapport with police. We don't need to advertise; people know us by word of mouth.

EU laws insisted that yard floors had to be covered in concrete so many shut down. Lots of laws came into existence. Liquids had to be put into drums. It cost me £30,000 to meet the requirements. I set up a unit to drain all the liquids out of the cars which we were dismantling.

Things Move on at the Yard

When I was extremely ill and in hospital, almost dying, Quinn and Marcus took over the business, like old hands. I was so proud of them. I just do the paperwork now.

I invented a car flattener, and had a furnace at the yard. When scrap prices fell to practically nothing, I got talking to a welder kid I knew, and we designed a car flattener on the back of a beer mat, in a pub. It took 18 months to complete. It worked brilliantly and flattened the cars to within six inches. I was that chuffed that I phoned BBC Look North. Harry Grayson commented on it when they sent a film crew out. They filmed Quinn and Marcus flattening the first car. It was a good bit of PR for the yard. One day when I was working the flattener, I banged the door behind me in my run-down office. It trapped my finger, and when I looked at my right hand, the tip of my middle finger just had a bone stuck up! I told my mate to get me a bit of rag because my finger tip was stuck on the door jar. I didn't faint, but he did! "Come on, get up, you've got to drive me to the hospital," I yelled. All the way there he wouldn't look at me, so I said, "You park up and I'll go inside and see if they can sew it back on. I'll be back at work tomorrow."

The nurse said, "Very sorry love, we can't sew that back on. It's dead now. We've got to file the bone down." So, I had to have an operation, I couldn't go home. My mate fell down on the floor again!

When I eventually got home it started hurting. I'd got a bit of gangrene in it, apparently. It was really, really painful and they had to file some more off! I used to play darts, and I was half-decent, but that put an end to that! Jack Sissons ran Hunslet Darts and Dominoes, so at least I could still play dominoes!

Sons Learn from Dad

When I took ill, my lads decided to close the yard on Sundays, because until then we were open seven days a week. I went ballistic, because most of our customers were working class and would come for parts on a weekend. The boys said, "We'll work it out, Dad. We're not going to end up ill like you did." Then the next thing I heard was that they were each having a week on and a week off, in a way.

One of the lads comes in three days and then the other! However, I admit my lads saw me struggle with my health, they saw me work every hour under the sun, so they are allowing themselves more 'me time', and enjoying their lives alongside their hard work.

Quinn is our gentle giant. His partner is an awesome American girl, Karen. Quinn loves cars, always has! As a toddler in our Kippax Street back-to-back, his favourite toy was a red plastic race car. He was always lying on the floor pretending to mend it! He has a white Porsche GT4

3.8 engine, a race car for the road! Only two hundred were produced, so he had to put a £5,000 deposit down. It's an investment. See, my lads know how to work hard but then play hard too!

One weekend, I couldn't get hold of Quinn. I always worry, it's in me! He was 50 but I still worried about him, and I said, "Where've you been?" He'd been doing a hovercraft test. Yes, he's bought one! He goes out to sea, on rivers and it can also go on land. Like his dad, he has always had the knack of making a bob or two in unconventional ways. He was spotted by a model agency once, and enjoyed a successful modelling career for a while!

My sons have both inherited my entrepreneur tendencies. Marcus bought a piece of land in Featherstone and put two semis on it, and purchased additional land by asking to buy the gardens of nearby houses. He erected more houses on it and called it Macaulay Place. Marcus rented them out and sold them all. Marcus has also built a swimming pool. You see, my lads like their leisure time but they are definitely grafters too! Marcus and his wife, who he married in Las Vegas, blessed us with the apple of our eye, Macaulay. We were fortunate to provide childcare for him for the first few years of his life. Whenever he sees us now, he always has a hug for us. Pat would invite all the neighbouring kids into the garden to play with him. Those kids grew up, and they still talk to us like old friends and call her Auntie Pat.

Macaulay's my hope to carry on our family name. I want to be around when I become a great-grandad! Our Macaulay got a motor track at Micklefield, something he always wanted to do. He's the one with brains in our family, having made us all proud with his school qualifications. He's a Parrish though, through and through, and his ambition, despite his paper qualifications, was to work at the yard. He made a huge success of the track too, getting bikers and their families up at weekends and holidays, even camping there! His kids' track was a complete hit. Karl Fogarty and three ex-world biking champions even hired Macaulay's track. Obviously, this information attracted even more customers.

Macaulay got into boxing. He arranged a fight with proceeds going to support a young widow and her family. He's got a good heart, our Macaulay. I've met boxer Barry McGuigan, I've met lots of famous people, but at the end of the day none of it matters; what really matters is my fantastic family. I just wish my mam was still alive to see all that my family and I have achieved.

For the Love of Cars

When Macaulay was just four years old, he drove himself into the record books! He thought it was fabulous when he got to drive his mini Mercedes SL pedal car for a quick test drive on the M1/A1 link road near Leeds, alongside me in my Mercedes E class. Don't worry, it was a newly completed stretch which hadn't yet opened to the public. I was in the lane next to him, and he was overtaking my Mercedes and killing himself laughing. At the end, I couldn't get him to stop!

"Oh grandad, I want to stay," he shouted, "Crash the car, crash the car!" He wanted to crash it into the barrier! I actually wrote to *Mercedes-Benz Magazine,* and they put it in the magazine. I think he'll always hold the record for the youngest driver ever on the M1 motorway!

Thinking Outside the Box

At a charity do I won a raffle bid to go on a tour of the *Emmerdale* set. I took eight business cards with me! You see, I like to think outside the box, use my initiative. I put them around everywhere! There was a pub on the set, and they often filmed shots of people talking on the telephone there.

I pinned one of my cards just behind where these shots were filmed, so hopefully it would show on a future filming!

The shop blew up on a future *Emmerdale* episode, and they had a notice board outside the shop. Of course, I'd pinned a card bang in the middle of this noticeboard. I never thought any more about it until suddenly my phone was red hot! "Leon, Leon, have you seen your card?" Apparently as the shop blew up, my card flew towards the camera!

I always look for unusual opportunities, and I have a great photo of Pat and I taken next to a clock at 12 minutes past 12 on the 12th of the 12th, 2012. We were out shopping, and I asked a complete stranger to take it. It'll be one hundred years before anyone can do it again!

My boys, Quinn and Marcus

Quinn's new toy

Macaulay Parrish, youngest ever driver on the M1 motorway

Me and Macaulay enjoying life

Photo taken on 12.12.12.12.12 – 12 minutes past 12 on 12/12/2012.
100 years before it'll happen again!

11. Family First

Pat's Birthdays

Pat and I don't go out with our own age group. Birthdays are just empty numbers for us, as Pat and I are young, mentally and physically, and we intend to stay that way for many more years! Seriously, all our friends are about 30 years younger than us. Maybe this is why we feel young!

When Pat was 40, I arranged a surprise party in Rothwell Men's Working Club, and I got all her friends to come. The place was packed: friends from holiday and school, and relatives. I'd told her we were just going for a meal with a couple of friends! Lights were down low, disco music playing, as she walked in. Lorraine, an old school friend greeted her as the Caribbean band started playing 'Happy Birthday'.

Pat asked that for her 50th birthday, instead of gifts, for friends to donate to the Yorkshire Evening Post's half and half appeal. Money was raised for Wheatfield's and St Gemma's hospice. She celebrated at the Lofthouse Hill Golf club. I arranged the surprise Caribbean band again, and a pig on a spit. How many 50-year-old women would look good in a pair of black hot pants, dancing on the table? My gorgeous gal looked stunning.

I always like to celebrate special events with Pat. For our golden wedding anniversary, we had a big do at a local club and celebrated on a cruise on Britannia. Kiki Dee was singing on it, and I asked for her to sing to Pat. She kept looking over and Pat said, "What's she looking at?" so I said that I had no idea. It turned out that Kiki couldn't believe we were old enough to have been married for 50 years, so she needed to check she'd got the right couple!

Super-Academy Scheme for Stars of the Future

I don't give up on a dream once it's entered my head. I wanted to share one such dream of mine with the football stars of the future, in Leeds. The centre of Middleton, on St George's field, saw my dream take root for boys and girls aged five to 17. I always aim high, and therefore I sought professional coaches who had gained experience from Leeds United and Manchester United. I won sponsorship for the red and white kit, and blue training tops. My tiered training plain ensured that all abilities were catered for.

Peter Lorimer came along to support us and offer advice and inspiration.

Talking of inspiration, what better motivation than St George himself attending the St George football academy just five weeks after it opened? Silly old gaffer that I am, I turned up dressed as, yes, St George. After all, I did want to make it a knight to remember! I was quite chuffed that we already had 11 teams registered with a loyal support network of parents!

My own 10-year-old grandson, Macaulay, made it a match to remember being named man of the match when his team won 4-0 and 3-1. I'll always remember his words, "I think this club is brilliant, Grandad. The facilities are much better than anywhere else." Our opening fun day was excellently attended. The footballers ran out to the presence of two knights in full armour from the royal armouries. A barbecue and music added to the brilliant atmosphere.

The football academy was absolutely amazing. Howard Wilkinson, ex-Leeds United manager, helped because he was very interested in my idea. He visited and sent his top trainer down there. This top trainer warned me against the coach we'd employed. I got a meeting with Leeds City council, and they were interested in giving me a grant to build an indoor football pitch similar to the Leeds United one at Thorpe Arch, and a room for parties and for premiership clubs to come along to check on the boys. All good stuff until the main guy who was training them up wasn't accepted by Leeds City council.

He must have upset them in the past, somehow. The message was delivered that they were sorry but, because of the coach I was in partnership with, they couldn't support us any further. That was it. A very good friend and I had already put £10,000 in each. Sadly, it all fell apart. However, all the lads went to Hunslet Boys Club and it's going well.

I have always tried to help the local football clubs because I know it is good for youngsters to run off their energy. I managed Rothwell Juniors for a while. I took over Marcus' under 10 team, and I used to put photos all over the inside of the van, not rude ones, just fun ones. I wanted to develop the team spirit as I drove the van to their matches. I did a few spins with the van for them!

If I go into my local pub nowadays, half a dozen of my old lads from that team will get on their knees and bow down to me, saying, "We are not worthy, we are not worthy!" We always had a laugh!

I've Got Lynne's Number

Yorkshire-born actress and Coronation Street star, Lynne Perrie, who played 'poisonous' Ivy Brennan gave her £10,000 personalised car number plate to me! I am just Lucky Leon! It was 8LP; I'd wanted it as soon as I spotted it, because Leon Parrish is the eldest of eight. I dropped her a line explaining that I'd be interested in buying the registration, and I had a figure of about two thousand pounds in mind, but for ages I didn't hear anything. Then she suddenly rang me out of the blue. We chatted for about forty minutes, and I told her I'd love to buy the plate from her. She then invited us to her home. Pat, who loves the soap, came with me and we spent three hours at Lynne's detached home in Salford. She was a great hostess and treated us like old friends. We drank flutes of champagne and buck's fizz.

I asked her if I could discuss a price for the plate, and she just gave me the log book and tax disc to send to the DVLA. We tried to give her some money but she wouldn't take it. She gave us a signed photo and wrote on it, "I hope the plates bring you luck." She was really comical, as she used to be a comedienne. I said, "You shouldn't have invited me round. I could have been a criminal for all you know!" I thought *I can't take this, I can't take this*, so I waited a couple of weeks and rang her back.

"I haven't put the registration plate on because you and my missus had enjoyed a couple of bottles of champagne, and you were both a bit tipsy, so I'm asking you now, will you accept payment, please?"

She said that, no, she didn't want anything. She claimed that she drank champagne regularly and was happy with her decision. She said that the reason she was giving it to me was because Pat and I had brought a light into her life. What a lovely, lovely lady, and I wrote to the paper to let everyone know what a kind person the poisonous Ivy was in real life!

Me and my girl in the Caribbean

We are sailing

Love this girl

Cruising

Knight of knight temple's

12. Fortune Hunting, Fortune Losing

Home Is Where the Heart Is

I won £1,030 on the football pools, back in the sixties. The Gaffer Above had helped me again because I had made a mistake and put two crosses in the wrong place, so my blunder made us win!

Three of us shared the winnings: my cousin, Billy, who I mentioned lived directly behind me, my friend Tony Battle and me! Sadly, Tony was another friend who got off my train early, as did his wife, Jean. Pat was disgruntled when we collected our winnings, and my mate gave his missus an open cheque to spend on the market. Pat tore up the fiver I gave her – I stuck it back together! I said we could pay for house essentials instead of just spending it all at once. Pat came round in the end, as she realised that we had to pay the mortgage off. I'd originally paid £250 for the back-to-back house, so I was delighted when we got £6,500 from the council who wanted to knock our palace down.

We bought a house in Leeds 10, but Pat didn't really settle there. We got a Barrett's box with the £6,500, and we lived there for nearly seven years. I've always bagged a bargain, so I managed to pay £16,500 for our next house which should have been 20 grand! At that time, I ran my man and a van business, and I'd bring home five hundred quid a week. Then the '80s depression came. I was struggling to pay the mortgage and realised that we had no option but to sell up. I put our house up for sale at £29,500, and the Gaffer Above helped me sell it within three days! Pat accepted that we had to live in a semi for a while. I said, "Don't worry love. We're buying this semi for £12,500 so we can pay the mortgage off, but I promise you I'll have you back in a detached house soon." I always keep my promises.

I had some great times as a man with a van! My mate, John Smith, had one arm shorter than the other, but he'd give me a hand. One day I carried a bed base into a house, and he was supposed to be carrying the mattress in after me. He never appeared. We were in hysterics when I found him, unable to move, as he couldn't get his arms up to release himself from being trapped underneath it! He later got a job at Tetley's, so Pat offered to help me. She put one of the kids' parkas on, and I said I'd share the tips with her. "Here's a quid for you and 50 pence for the lad," one customer said. She was carrying a bed end, and the wind blew her into the bushes. Not sure if she was most mad about the fact that she'd been taken for a lad, the small tip or the humiliation of ending up on her backside!

Sometimes my kids helped me out. I just needed to stare at them and they'd know to behave. They were cracking kids, not a bit of trouble. When I was a man with a van, they used to come with me, delivering newspapers round Wetherby. At Boston Spa, one of the shopkeepers always had a bag of sweets ready for them.

The House That Pat and Leon Built

Pat and I have built a lifetime together, never mind a house. My Pat was sprinkled with angel dust from the Gaffer Above. Even in her seventies, she's still beautiful. We came from an age where you marry for life. I just wish that all those years ago my mam could have seen into the future, and seen the house Pat and I built and the grand way that Pat furnished it. Mind you, she'd had practise, as we had eight houses before this one!

It was when I bought an old farmhouse that Pat got in on the act of fame. When we built a new house on the garden at the side, Pat did all the interior design. I put Pat's name forward for a competition in the *Yorkshire Post,* and she gave me a right rollicking when I told her! She had to get her own designs, and she made our house look amazing.

She won. They asked her if she wanted them to put her forward for business, but she refused, saying that she'd just done it for fun!

Later, I got a team together and built a house on the land at the back of the house. I had no experience of building houses, but I'm a good manager. I half designed it myself, all the inside was hardwood. It cost me £48,000 to build but I already had the land. A house truly fit for a lord, with the minstrel's gallery, the ceiling roses and a beautiful grey marble fireplace. Reuben-style murals adorned the staircase walls. Cherubs and clouds reflected the angel theme that seems to have been present through my life. Marble floors, gold-leaf Japanese screens, and a gold-plated bathroom all adorned the house designed by patient Pat.

We built it on a former mushroom farm. We dug out the footings, and good friends in the building trade helped out. When we ran out of cash at one stage, we had to lock the building up for several months.

One Christmas we went away to Lanzarote, and when we were coming back, we got a phone call from Quinn telling us not to bother coming home! "Go to a hotel," he said, "You've had a flood!"

It was like Noah's ark! A pipe in the loft had burst. Water had brought all the ceilings down. It was the postman who'd noticed floating letters! It was a horrendous time, we ended up going to Oulton Hall hotel for two weeks and then rented a little house. The insurance company said it would take three years to put right, so I said I'd do it myself with a band of people. It took me nine months. Pat was obviously heartbroken after all her hard work.

Once a Builder, Always a Builder!

I was talking with Pat the other day, and I wondered how we managed to do what we did, me and my lass? We were always up to something! In an auction I bought an old library, opposite from the Robin Hood pub. I bid 20 grand for it and, to my astonishment, I got it! I built a block of three flats. Quinn moved into the penthouse for a while. I'm proud that it bears the name "Parrish Mews 2006."

I still own them, and I keep them well decorated, charging decent rents. If I could find some land I'd love to build some more!

13. Knowing Me

My Hero, Sir James Goldsmith

Sir James Goldsmith, the late billionaire leader of the Referendum Party, was my hero. I wanted to be English, not European! I consider myself very lucky and privileged to have worked for and with Sir James Goldsmith; a true gentleman and patriot of Britain with tremendous love for his fellow man. Sir James's death was a sad loss to all who worked for him and to everyone in Britain. I believed that the common market was good, but the EU was wrong. Goldsmith was such a powerful speaker who made one stand up with pride, and put tears in your eyes.

I stood for the Referendum Party in Leeds East. In my constituency, I was facing George Mudie of the Labour Party who got a majority of 17,000. I was late to join the game, but after just six months I managed 1,267 votes. How did I get involved? Well, I simply read a leaflet and rang the head office for more information. Next thing you know, I'd been asked to stand for the party. As you will be starting to recognise, I always find a way! So determinedly I spent hours, on the night before the election, going round all the forty-seven polling stations in my constituency, putting up posters asking for the constituents' votes. The next morning, they were all down, replaced by posters from the Labour party. I really stood for my sons and grandson. I was proud to stand, and to show that the ordinary working man can campaign.

I had a lorry outside the party's regional offices in Guiseley. I had a big billboard on the back and stickers: "Britannia doesn't rule, ok?" When we were at the conference in London, I met up with an old friend who had lost half his stomach at Arnhem. He was a Chelsea Pensioner, Tony Battle, a sergeant in the Paras. He told me he was counting on me. I'm British and proud of it. I fought like mad for us to come out of Europe. Sir James Goldsmith, my hero in life, put 20 million pounds of his own money in to start the Referendum Party. He gave me Seacroft, three weeks before the election, as I really did want out of Europe because I was a true Brexiteer. I think Boris is an excellent prime minister. Pat says I should have been prime minister!

Everyone who stood was treated to a holiday In Majorca. We met all the other candidates. I met a bloke there who was already a councillor for Leeds city council, and he asked where I lived. When I said, Rothwell, he told me he was from Methley! Yes, he's the man I bought my title from!

What Annoys Smiley Miley?

Someone asked me if anything makes me mad, and I had to think carefully, as usually I have a laid-back approach to life! Lazy people annoy me. The green-eyed monster in people annoys me. My missus and me have grafted for everything we've done, so nobody should be jealous of us! We love people, we love to laugh and joke, so I'd be annoyed if I had to live in the countryside and not see others, but having said that, I coped well with isolation through the 2020 virus lockdown, and became a star cleaner with Pat!

I'm not annoyed by things that annoy lot of people; for example, I'm not bothered by traffic jams. I just look at all those cars and see work for my lads! Leeds United not going up annoyed me!

I detest people who are cruel to kids, but I always think karma will get them in the end. I met Jimmy Saville before the truth came out, and when it did Sky TV filmed my anger at his deeds as I tore up a card he'd once sent to Pat and me. Not long after his funeral, and before any of us discovered what he'd done, his family put an auction up for his memorabilia, and I bid for his Rolls Royce. The estimate was £80,000 but the bidding went frantic. I stopped at £120,000. It went for 125 grand, coincidentally to a scrap man. He obviously lost all his money when the truth came out, because nobody wanted that car. Lucky Leon, again; the Gaffer's angels were looking after me!

I scream down the phone at cold callers and teach them a bit of Yorkshire language! They annoy me!

Four Words to Sum Me Up?

I was asked for four words which described me. "Short, fat, bald and ugly. LOL," was my answer!

Others have more kindly said, "Helpful, selfless, energetic and witty." I'm sure they meant, twitty!

Cruising

We tried land holidays and gave a campervan a go! It had a little scooter on the back. We drove through Spain, and camped in Benidorm. The plan was to drive on to Italy, but Pat decided the camping life wasn't for her; and Pat is the boss, so that was the end of that!

We absolutely love cruising. Ever since Pat was 47, we've never been happier than on the ocean waves. Mind you, I did have to fork out for a new cruise wardrobe for her! The staff is amazing, staff like Paul Brown, a captain on P & O, the company we always choose. We don't like land holidays anymore, we find them boring compared to cruises. Everything on a cruise is amazing, and we're so lucky to be able to do it. We love the Caribbean.

On one cruise we met a taxi driver on St Kitts who befriended us and took us to his house for meals. We saw his children grow up as we visited him year after year. We make so many friends, every single cruise, and we embrace the nightlife. Folk try to book their next cruise just to spend time with us again, honest! So much fun, laughter, and partying 'til the early hours. This is LIFE, as it should be!

So many amazing friends, like Christopher and Liz Lane who put toffee in the vodka shots for the best New Year's ever were on board! Up on the top deck they rearranged the tables and practically became the official bar! They served the staff entertainers, so they certainly gave us some laughs from the stage!

My Adopted Daughter

"When we arrived at the resort you were strangers, and by the time we left you were special friends. It would make us so happy if you were to visit us over here, on this side of the pond."

Special words from my adopted daughter and her husband! "To our English angels," was written on the back of their thank you letter, and I thank the Gaffer Above for my day as dad to a daughter!

You see, two years ago we met a lovely couple. We were in the Bahamas at Sandals, not a cruise! I went for breakfast while Pat was having a lie in, and I saw a bloke with a Leeds United shirt on. You have to sit beside a fellow fan! "Hey up man, we won last night!" I greeted him.

"I'm not a Leeds United supporter!"

"What do you mean?"

"I'm from Canada. and a friend gave me this,"

"I bet he's a Man United supporter,"

"How did you know?"

"Because your friend has said 'wear this' for a laugh! Listen, you've got a shirt on of the best supporting club in the world, you be proud of that."

I asked if he was with family and he said no, just him and his girl. He went on to explain that they were getting married on this holiday. I asked who was giving her away, and he said a member of staff. I haven't got any daughters, so it was a privilege to offer my services. We got treasured photos with Sandy and my adopted daughter for the day, Samantha. We got on as if we'd known them all our life. Samantha looked stunning, and I started blubbering; a proper adopted dad! Sandy went into politics, he's doing well. They have two daughters now and, who knows, I might go over and surprise them one day!

Tie a Yellow Ribbon

Ever since I heard that the French said the British oak is a poisonous tree, that it should be killed off, as a true Brit I decided to gather acorns. I've planted them everywhere; in farmers' fields, on country walks. I even snuck some abroad into France to show them! Spanish botanical gardens will be wondering how the oaks got there!

As you know, I got permission for one behind mam's headstone. When Auntie Louie, mam's sister, was dying in hospital, she was over the moon when I said she could go in the grave with my mam. They went everywhere together, joined at the hip. She used to sing when my mam played the piano. Just before Lou died, she started singing, 'Tie a yellow ribbon round the old oak tree'. We all started singing with her as she passed away. At the bottom of the headstone,

I had a piano engraved for my mam. There is always a yellow ribbon around my oak now for Auntie Louie. The other brothers used to meet up with my mam every Sunday morning for bacon sandwiches and a singsong. She loved the full house. I like to think I have created the perfect resting place for mam and Auntie Lou, and one day she'll have a full house again when I get laid to rest there too!

Things the Boy in the Tin Bath Would Never Have Believed

That boy, Leon, sitting in the tin bath in that old front room, would have been amazed if he could have looked into the future and seen what he's achieved with the blessings from the Gaffer Above. That boy had always said to his mam, "I'll have my own house with a bath in it and it'll be posh."

When my mam died, I'd only just begun to make decent money in the yard. I wish I'd been able to take her on a few good cruises; that is a sad regret, even today, for me. An old friend, Colin Wilson, nicknamed Winkie used to go round pubs mending fruit machines. He loved my mam and Louie, and he told me that if she'd been alive today, she'd be so proud of me, and that her and Louie will be partying up there, proud of me. That meant the world to me.

The eyes of that boy in the bath would pop out if they could see me in the Waldorf, sitting in the rocking chair once owned by President Kennedy! From sitting in a mucky Hunslet bath to sitting in the President's rocking chair! I've lived it up, sailing to New York, staying in the Waldorf for a whole week. Pat and I were having a nosey round when we discovered the presidential suite. We bribed the maid to let us have a little venture inside! General MacArthur's desk was there too.

There was a massive ballroom in the Waldorf. I could almost feel the eyes of the boy from the tin bath watching me as I danced with my Pat where presidents had danced.

We met a famous basketball team staying there! I bought a pair of below-knee shorts and a basketball top. The place was in uproar when dwarf me, attired in full kit, stood with those players!

I took an England flag, which all the lads from the Sun pub in Hunslet had signed, to the site of the twin towers. A crowd of Americans clapped as I hung it to show our respect. The boy in the tin bath would have swooned to know.

I visited Graceland driving in a soft-top red sports car. Click, click, click went my camera as we completed the tour, listening on headphones to recordings of Elvis chatting with his friends. I bought a gold record there, Elvis is back'. It's number 44 out of 500. Staying in the hotel at Memphis was very nostalgic as they played Elvis music all night. At Sun City studios, I sang into the very same microphone that Elvis used; such an amazing feeling for me!

Tin bath boy would not have dreamt that one day he might be considering buying a Rolls Royce Cullinan. Pat and I went for a test run in the £350,000 dream. Pat's feet wouldn't touch the floor so Patrick, the salesman, pushed a button and a footrest came up. We went down to stay in a stately hall on a Rolls Royce experience day. We got to drive a Cullinan at 150 miles per hour. The cream-coloured Cullinan tempts me still, so that boy in the tin bath might get to own one, but for now I'll stick to my Bentleys, a 4x4 Bentayga and a W12 GTC (207mph). Yay!

I'm sure he'd like to see my Bentley book. There were 100 of them, all numbered. Prince Charles has the number one copy, and he had donated hide to cover two of the books. Lucky Leon has number three, one of the covered books! How did I get it? The registration of my Bentley GTC was THE 800K which obviously could look like THE BOOK. It was a great advertising ploy to use my reg and as a reward for lending it I got my book! I have also got an OPUS book, The Final Round no. 12, Muhammad Ali. There are three photos of Ali taken just six weeks before he died. Both books are collectors' items and I treasure them.

We have so many treasured memories. Pat and I flew on Concorde, an amazing experience. Massive leg room space, meals on china plates with steel knives and forks. Champagne glasses full, no murmur, so smooth! We landed in Barcelona. We cruised back home on Queen Elizabeth.

The trip included a stay in the New Forest, horse riding and then an Orient Express train home. Cath Simms, a dear friend, suggested the trip.

Telly Star

Wherever I go, I seem to end up on television or in the newspapers! I went to Vegas to watch boxing, Tyson against Frank Bruno, and they interviewed me. The next morning, a mate ran up and asked me if I'd seen that I was on the front page. He ran over, and bought all the papers back from one of the machines. I had to put them back so I wouldn't get arrested! Our Quinn was back in England, having a shave, and he heard the voice of his old man on the telly!

Once we took our wives on a foreign football trip. Pat came running up to me and said, "I believe you now."

I said, "Believe what?"

She said, "The cameras come to you, not you to them!" She said she'd just gone round the corner ahead with her pals, and the camera crew were lurking. She heard them say they were just waiting for the bloke with the hat on! It was an Australian bush hat with corks on! They followed us down the arcade, and tried to come into the sports shop with us so I told them to stop right there, that they couldn't come into the sports shop with because we couldn't do any shoplifting if they were there! They were loving my jesting, especially when I photographed them filming us! When we got back to the hotel the receptionist said, "You're famous all over Italy." I should have been a film star!

Number one Brexiteer

My adopted daughter for the day, Samantha, and her new hubby Sandy

US President John F. Kennedy's rocking chair, which I sat in

My Patricia sat at General MacArthur's desk

The book, showing Chris and Liz Lane

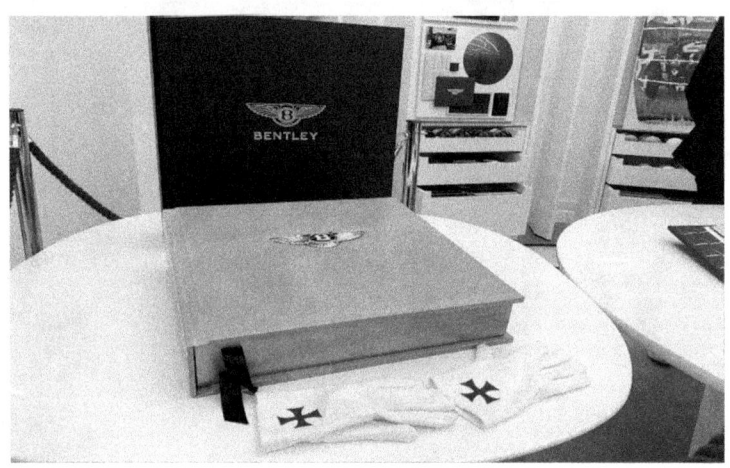

The book, number three out of 100!

From tin bath to GTC Bentley. The don!

Lovebirds

14. Communication

Thank You for Being the Reason I Smile

I keep scrapbooks, mainly to pass on to my grandson, Macaulay. They include all sorts of memorabilia from my life, but some of the contents are the numerous thank you cards I've received over the years. They are very precious to me. A few quotes from them which have meant the world to me and Pat follow:

"You really are two of life's angels."

"We look on you as part of our family."

"You guys definitely made our vacation an unforgettable one."

"The two of you always put a smile on our faces."

"Very rarely do we have the opportunity to meet people who are so genuine and caring."

"There are numerous occasions when your names will come up and it is always accompanied by a smile."

"You guys rock."

"I could never thank you enough for all that you have done for me."

"There are very few people in this world that are as brave, sincere and kind as you two."

"True friends are very few and far between."

"You have been really good friends to us and you really do understand me."

"We loved your company and great chats each night. Who needs entertainment when Leon is around? He is one of life's precious gifts."

My mate, Martin Gold, a comic, was an exceptionally good son to his mum, Irene. He bought a house in Miami but he was still down to earth. He told me that his mum once said if she ever needed anything, the one man she'd turn to was Leon, "He's the only guy that I would trust." I thought that was really nice. I once bought an old Rolls-Royce Silver Shadow II. I was going to use it for weddings but I never did, so I sold it. He told me that he saw me driving in it at the time and I was his inspiration, that he wanted to be like Leon!

The Dinosaur Gets Techy

I was on holiday yet again! Woodrow 'Woody' Janvier, an American, and I were watching football, an England game. Woody sat next to me and he took his flip flop off, and flipped the top off his bottle. Amazing, underneath the sole was a bottle opener! He asked me what size my flip flops were and we swapped so we both had a bottle opener! He asked if I was on Facebook. I'd never heard of it and wasn't interested until he said the magical phrase, "It's free!" That phrase always makes a Yorkshire man prick up his ears, and I was hooked! I now use WhatsApp and Facebook all the time! I'm still in contact with Woody and his missus, Kirsten, on Facebook. Great people.

15. Content with Life

From Tin Bath to Marble Bath

I have never lost the small joys of life enjoyed by the boy in the tin bath, even though I have been fortunate to experience such amazing times. Now, as the man in the marble bath, I know that I am content with my life, and that is a blessing greater than any of my riches. Pat and I love each other's company.

Pat and I enjoy the compliments we still receive these days, that we look young and fit for our age. I never once touched a drug, except in hospital given by doctors. Yuck! I love life, I didn't ever need to rely on a boost from a drink or a drug. Don't get me wrong, we love our nights out still. We particularly enjoy the gay scene in Leeds, the music and the atmosphere are electric! Great fun times, great people.

We've never gone to a gym; we enjoy our daily walks with the local farm dogs. They scream when they see us, and they always obey their recall, unless they are chasing a hare! Animals are brilliant, sometimes better than people.

Remember Me

I'd like to be remembered above all for being a trier and a family man, and I hope that people might say the world would have been a duller place without me. I tried. I've done my best. Above all, always smile and be happy, even if the smile sometimes hides pain.

I still have plans to live to a very old age, to continue to cruise the Caribbean, to hold a great grandchild – and will you find me driving that cream Cullinan around Rothwell, either in my dreams or in reality? You'll have to read my next book to discover the answer to that one!

My Personal Message to You

Life is like a journey on a train, with all its stations, with all its changes of routes and with accidents along the way. At birth we board, meet our parents and believe they will always travel by our side. However, at some station they will step down, leaving us on the journey alone. As stations fly past, other folk will join the train, our siblings, friends, the love of our lives and our children. Many will disembark, leaving a permanent vacuum. We won't notice others vacate their seats. The journey will be full of joy, sorrow, fantasy, expectations, hellos and farewells. Success consists of having a good relationship with all the passengers, requiring that we give the best of ourselves.

The mystery is that we don't know which station we, ourselves, will get off at, so we must live in the best possible way, sharing love and forgiveness and the best of who we are. When we leave our seat empty, we should leave behind beautiful memories for those who will follow and travel on the train of life. To all who got off at an earlier stop, we'll meet again, I promise.

I wish you all a successful journey. Most importantly give thanks for the journey, as I do, to the Gaffer Above, not forgetting my angels.

I thank you all for being passengers on my train. Keep smiling :)

Leon Michael Davies Parrish.

Proud granddad

CPSIA information can be obtained
at www.ICGtesting.com
Printed in the USA
BVHW031355290422
635742BV00011B/401

9 781398 438897